To Christopher —

Merry Christmas
1970

Love,
Aunt Annette

FOREWORD

Many books have been written about the United Nations. Some good. Some not. Most of them for adult readers. I welcome this book especially because it is different in its aim. It seeks to tell the story of the United Nations for the youngest readers. It is an interesting, even a thrilling story for readers of any age. By its words and its pictures, set forth in clear and simple terms and lines, this book, I believe, catches very much of the meaning of the United Nations.

I feel that this little volume will achieve its purpose. It is not, I am sure, beyond the ken of a child, even a very young one, to understand and to know something about living at peace with one's neighbors and in one's surroundings, about elemental justice and the hurt of injustice, about one's own rights and respecting the rights of others, and about helping those around us who are in sore need of help. The young readers of this book know about such things in their play relations and in their relations with the adults surrounding them. Indeed, young ones at times appear to be more sensitive to matters of this kind than some of their elders. This book will give its young readers a broader — an international — setting for their thinking and thereby help to widen the reader's horizon. In these critical times the facts of international life need to be taught at the tenderest age.

Certainly no reader has a greater stake in the United Nations than those youngest ones who will peruse this book, with entire lives ahead of them in a world which is unlikely to survive unless the United Nations can preserve peace in it.

RALPH J. BUNCHE
Under-Secretary for Special Political Affairs
United Nations

LET'S FIND OUT ABOUT

THE UNITED NATIONS

by

MARTHA and CHARLES SHAPP

Pictures by Angela Conner

FRANKLIN WATTS, INC.
575 Lexington Avenue, New York 22

Library of Congress Catalog Card Number: 61-11333
Printed in the United States of America

7   8   9

We live in a big, big world.

There are many different countries in this big world.

Many people live in these countries.
In some ways, the people of different
countries are different.

 Some people look different.

Some dress differently.

Some speak different languages.

But people are alike in more ways than they are different.

All people need food.

All people need homes.

All people work.

All over the world . . .

. . people like to dance and sing.

Most of the time, the nations of the world, like people in a big family, get along together.

But sometimes, like people in a big family, they disagree.
Sometimes when people in a family disagree, they get angry
and fight.

Sometimes nations disagree and fight.

When nations fight, it is called war.

War is sad.

War is terrible.

The leaders of some nations decided to try to stop wars.

They said, "Let's get together. Let's unite. Let's talk things over instead of fighting."

These nations united and became the UNITED NATION
The UNITED NATIONS building is in New York.

The flags of all the UNITED NATIONS
stand in front of the U.N.
(The letters U.N. stand for UNITED NATIONS.)

Now when nations in the U.N. disagree
they talk things over instead of fighting.

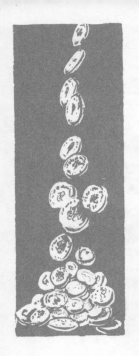

The U.N. works in many ways to help the people of the world.

Sometimes, the U.N. sends money and tools.

Sometimes, the U.N. sends people to teach better ways of
  doing things.

With this help, the people in these countries can build better
roads, homes, and schools.

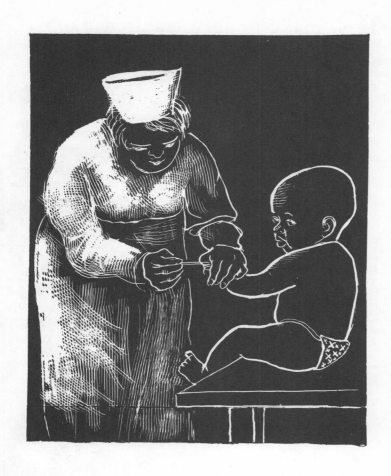

The U.N. sends doctors and nurses to teach
people how to keep healthy.

You can help the U.N. make hungry children happy.

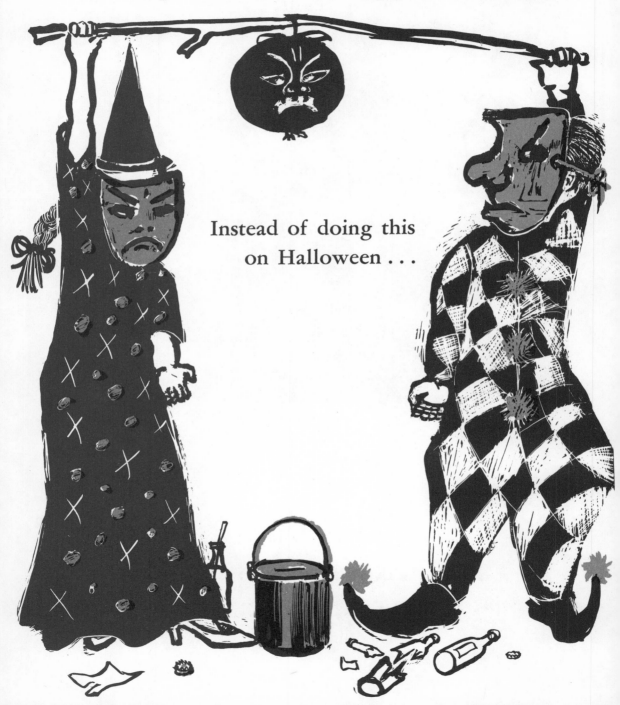

Instead of doing this
on Halloween . . .

. . . you can do this.

Send the money you collect to the U.N. to help the hungry children of the world.

The world is a family of nations.

The U.N. is the home of this big family.

VOCABULARY LIST (99 words)

a
alike
all
along
and
angry
are

became
better
big
build(ing)
but

called
can
children
collect
countries

dance
decided
different(ly)
disagree
do(ing)
doctors
dress

family
fight(ing)
flags
food
for
front

get

Halloween
happy

healthy
help
home(s)
how
hungry

in
instead
is
it

keep

languages
leaders
let's
letters
like
live
look

make
many
money
more
most

nations
need
New York
now
nurses

of
on
over

people

roads

sad
said
schools
send(s)
sing
some
sometimes
speak
stand
stop

talk
teach
terrible
than
the
there
these
they
things
this
time
to
together
tools
try

unite(d)

war(s)
way(s)
we
when
with
work(s)
world

you

The LET'S FIND OUT Books

by MARTHA and CHARLES SHAPP

LET'S FIND OUT ABOUT ANIMAL HOMES
LET'S FIND OUT WHAT'S BIG AND WHAT'S SMALL
LET'S FIND OUT WHAT ELECTRICITY DOES
LET'S FIND OUT ABOUT FIREMEN
LET'S FIND OUT ABOUT HOUSES
LET'S FIND OUT ABOUT INDIANS
LET'S FIND OUT WHAT'S LIGHT AND WHAT'S HEAVY
LET'S FIND OUT ABOUT POLICEMEN
LET'S FIND OUT ABOUT SCHOOL
LET'S FIND OUT WHAT THE SIGNS SAY
LET'S FIND OUT WHAT'S IN THE SKY
LET'S FIND OUT ABOUT THE UNITED NATIONS
LET'S FIND OUT ABOUT WATER
LET'S FIND OUT ABOUT WHEELS

and

LET'S FIND OUT ABOUT SPRING
LET'S FIND OUT ABOUT SUMMER
LET'S FIND OUT ABOUT FALL
LET'S FIND OUT ABOUT WINTER